Networking MASTERY

THE UNFAIR ADVANTAGE OF BUILDING CONNECTIONS FOR CAREER & LIFE ACCELERATION IN THE MODERN WORLD

by Charity Majors

Copyright © 2025 by Charity Majors

All rights reserved.

No portion of this book may be reproduced in any form without written permission from the publisher or author, except as permitted by U.S. copyright law.

Published by Arise Publishing House

ArisePublishingHouse.com

Contents

What they said...Praise for "Networking Mastery"	1
1. WHY Networking? (It's not what you think)...	2
2. The Mindset of a Master Networker	9
3. Understanding Your Networking Goals	22
4. The Art of First Impressions	28
5. Building Your Network Strategically	40
6. Leveraging Technology for Networking Success	48
7. The Power of Giving in Networking	57
8. Maintaining and Nurturing Relationships	69
9. Shift the Networking Culture with Us!	77
10. About Charity Majors	79
Learn more at CharityMajors.com	
11. Acknowledgements	82

What they said...Praise for "Networking Mastery"

Joanne
★★★★★ **Must read if you want to grow your network**
Reviewed in the United States on December 30, 2024
I've been to Charity's workshops and this book nails it! If you're not networking intentionally, you're missing out. Solid must read from one of the best coaches in connecting.

Jon
★★★★★ **"Mastery" says it all**
Reviewed in the United States on December 30, 2024
I've had the privilege of being part of one of Charity's in-person networking events and she commands this space! This book covers so many key practices and elements that make her style shine!

Chelsea Husum
★★★★★ **So excited for this book!!**
Reviewed in the United States on December 31, 2024
I'm loving this book so far!! Charity gives such powerful nuggets and actionable advice for anyone looking to make deeper more authentic connections!

Amy B.
★★★★★ **Great advice**
Reviewed in the United States on December 30, 2024
What a great book filled with valuable nuggets on networking. I had so many take aways that I'm looking forward to implementing.

Dina M Cerchione
★★★★★ **Informative AND Heart centered**
Reviewed in the United States on December 30, 2024
Verified Purchase
If you want to learn how to network in a way that feels authentic but not "ick" and leads to results this is the book for you!

Lai G
★★★★★ **Invaluable resource!**
Reviewed in the United States on December 30, 2024
Verified Purchase
They say your network is your net-worth and this book is an invaluable resource for networking with authenticity and impact.

Chapter One

WHY Networking? (It's not what you think)...

Before we start, I want to give you a gift. Go to BusinessAndBubbly.com/questions and grab my list of 50 of the best questions that help you create genuine connection. You're going to need them as you dive into the world of networking...It's a $47 value that I want to give you for FREE so go to the website and download them really quick before we dive in...

Now that you've gotten them, let's get started...

Welcome to the place where connections become catalysts and potential becomes performance in order to make a major impact.

Hi, I'm Charity Majors and I believe that in today's digital age, cultivating quality connections is one of the most valuable skills we can develop so get good at it now and stick with it for the long haul. It will be *the unfair advantage* you'll have over everyone else, whether you want to advance in business or life.

Maybe you, like me, heard all sorts of great things about networking and making connections but you had a similar experience. Maybe you've done some networking and can see the value in it but you're ready to take things up a notch (or 10). Or maybe you're leading a networking community and you're ready to learn advanced ways to not just network yourself but empower those around you to become even better networkers and connectors.

Wherever you're at in your journey, know that you're in the right place. This book is meant to be a guide as you go from the awkward newbie into a master connector or even leader of a networking group because this is a part of my story too.

I *was* the awkward new girl that stuck with something long enough to not just become a master connector but to create a nationwide networking company that shifted the industry from boring beige conference rooms, bad 30-second elevator pitches and surface conversations into thriving communities driven by purpose, genuine quality connection, trust, growth and having FUN together whether it's for business or in life.

> Our motto says *"we rally around the genuine belief that we are better together and together, we can show the world what's possible."*

Throughout my journey, I've learned a lot about what *not* to do as well as what works really really well and I'm going to pass along those lessons. I've gone to the shy girl so afraid to say anything to anyone to using connections that got me on stage speaking along side major leaders and influencers, now with a company that is literally founded upon connection and community.

Did you know that 2 out of 3 people report being lonely? 70% of leaders report being lonely. And the Surgeon General recently released an 83 page document declaring that we are in an epidemic of loneliness, which is worse for our health than heart disease and diabetes.

Our culture values independence, convenience and privacy more than they value community and connection (or at least that's what our actions show).

We have garage doors on the front of our houses instead of porches. We have common sayings like "it's lonely at the top" instead of having the mentality of bringing people to the top with us. We have tall fences that keep people out instead of short gates that invite people to be a part of our lives. We don't know our neighbors and would rather order Instacart over asking the lady next door for some eggs when we run out. We choose what's convenient and comfortable over the inconvenience of getting together with others on a regular basis.

If you are feeling the ache of lonliness, I want to be the first to let you know that there's actually nothing wrong with you! That's right...there's *nothing* wrong with you. Just like our physical body has signals that let us know we're in pain and something is wrong, so does our soul – our mind, will and emotions. If you're feeling lonely, that's actually a sign that your soul is craving connection, so congratulations, you're working correctly! Now it's up to you to find those that you can connect with to help. Being a part of community is a sign of a healthy soul, so let's help get your heart what it needs.

Now, maybe this isn't you, but you better believe it's the person you're sitting next to in the office, it's the teller at your bank, or the parents on your kids sports teams. It's more than half of your team members and those sitting in the rows at Church. It's the majority of your "friends" on social media, despite what their polished profile portrays.

The truth is, is that this "disconnection dilelma" effects *all* of us as a collective and I'm on a mission to provide a solution for this, because I know what the solution is.

It's **connection.**

One of the ways we can create connections is by networking. Now, I know what you're thinking...*networking?? Ick...* Yes, networking, *but* not in the way you may know it to be and how it's always been done. I'm writing this book in an effort to bring the concept of networking out of the 1980's and into a modern world that needs connection and community more than ever.

I went from the awkward networker feeling awkward in the corner of the room into a super connector who not only has incredible and powerful global connections, but I've also created deep and meaningful friendships and incredible community out of the "vehicle" of networking. It changed my life so much that I felt so compelled to start a company that is founded upon networking and cultivating genuine connection because I truly believe that when done right, *"you're just one connection away..."* and that *this* is the solution our disconnected and highly digitized world is so desperately needing right now.

As I have unpacked the gift of connection in my own life and now the lives of hundreds of women around the country, it's now my job to pass that onto even more people, just like you.

Charity Majors speaking about finding, developing and giving what you've learned along the way.

Just like this quote in this picture says, "the purpose of life is to discover your gift. The work of life is to develop it. The meaning of life is to give your gift away." (author unknown). Part of the greater call on my life is to not just be connected myself, but to show others the way and this book is a small part of that...

Being on this mission, I'm also aware that we have a long way to go in a rapidly increasing world of digital worlds that only lead us into superficial connection. The truth is, is that nothing replaces the magic of genuine connection, especially heart to heart, soul to soul, business to business, belly to belly, connection.

Not only are we swimming against the current of the disconnected digital age, there's also a current of "networking how it's always been done...". Now, don't get me wrong, there's wisdom in ways that work, *and* the world has shifted in a way that requires entire industries to shift as well. And networking is one of them.

In order too shift the culture of something that's been done how it's been done for decades, I also know that I can't shift culture alone. My hope is that this book invites you into not just *"networking how its always been done"*, or to stay with the convenience of social media "friends" all the while your soul is aching with loneliness, but to invite you into deeper understanding of creating connections that will help heal lonely hearts. Not only that, but to help be a part of the solution that the human race is craving during this time in history.

Networking is about Connection.
And connection will help heal the world.
Because we were created for community.
Now let's dive in… are you with me?!… Let's go…

Chapter Two

The Mindset of a Master Networker

I walked into a room full of strangers feeling uncomfortable and out of place. I scanned the boring beige conference room looking for even just one familiar face and found none. After signing in at the registration table and sticking the ugly "Hello, my name is" name tag to my shirt, I sheepishly wandered over to the table with sips and snacks, hoping to find some water for my mouth that had dried up because I was so nervous.

As I fumbled around the snack table filled with cheap salty food, having a few awkward surface conversations and all started with the boring "so, what do you do" question and mentions about the weather, having a handful of business cards shoved in my hands and elevator sales pitches that left me feeling like this was a fluorescent room filled with salty-salesmen, I wondered why so many people raved on and on about creating connections and networking because if *this* was what it was, *no thanks*...

After finishing my salty snacks in that boring beige conference room and making it out of the awkward conversations alive, I found my seat at the cold brown table. I listened as the leader of the networking event shared how to do the 30-second elevator pitch and watched as person after person robotically regurgitated what they did in their business.

"My name is so-and-so. The name of my business is such-and-such. I do yadda-yadda."

Then, it was my turn...

I took another sip of water to help my dry mouth. I stood and pushed my chair back, which made a squeaking noise that filled the entire room. I cleared my throat, looked around the room at all of the unfamiliar faces, took a deep breath, and spoke...

"My name is Charity and I believe that health is one of the greatest gifts we can give ourselves and others. I do this through my wellness company which helps people achieve health and vitality so they can live healthy lives. I'm a personal trainer, nutrition specialists, and my company and boutique fitness studio is called "Boise Fitness Factory." (this was many many years ago with a former business I had that got me in the door of networking)...

After I finished sharing my "pitch," the room got silent. I sat back down not knowing if what I said landed with anyone because I didn't follow directions of the typical elevator pitch. What I said wasn't the normal robotic elevator pitch...it *felt* different...inspiring, filled with passion and life, unlike the monotone robotic pitches we'd all been hearing and slowly lulled to sleep by.

I remember looking around at all of the unfamiliar faces who had gone from what looked like death-by-boredom into bright-eyed smiles and there was a new sense of *life* in that boring beige meeting room.

After the meeting ended, I had people lining up to meet me, to connect with me, and even had a few people book appointments at my business, who shortly after turned into customers. I received multiple referrals and was invited back not just as a member, but *as a speaker*.

Walking to my car that day, I realized I was on to something. I had shifted the culture of that room and I was determined to figure out how to do it again and again not just for myself, but because the world had shifted. Business had shifted. Things were different in this digital age and new generations were entering the workforce. But somehow, networking meetings had stayed in the past.

What caused the shift I made in the room? Let's find out...

Networking is often perceived as a series of transactional exchanges, an obligatory dance at professional gatherings where business cards are exchanged and small talk fills the air in boring beige conference rooms. However, to truly excel in networking in today's modern world, you have to embrace a fundamental shift in perspective—viewing it not only as a means to an end but as an opportunity for genuine relationship-building. This chapter will explore how adopting this mindset can lead to more meaningful connections and ultimately propel your career and life forward.

The name "networking" comes with some interesting preconceived notions as to what it is. But to truly become a master networker, we've got to get rid of some of the false (and old) beliefs.

At its core, **networking is about cultivating relationships** that can enrich both your personal and professional life. When you approach networking with the intention of building connections rather than just seeking out quick benefits, you open yourself up to deeper interactions that can give far greater returns over time. Think of it as planting seeds in a garden; with patience and care, these seeds can grow into fruitful partnerships that benefit everyone involved.

As the founder and leader of a nationwide networking company, trust me when I say that those who come in to quickly pop in and pop out of a networking group to exploit it can be spotted a mile away. They come in, talking only about themselves and their business, and most of what they do is "take" from the people they meet.

On the other hand, those who come into a networking community with the intention to build relational equity - that "*connection capital*" and make connections over time are the ones who receive the biggest return on investment. I like to invite our members to "***not just be in community, but to let community be in you***". Just like there's a difference between being in the ocean and taking a drink of water, when you let community "be in you" just like when you take a drink of water, it will help nourish you on a deeper level than simply being in the ocean.

Another analogy besides water and a garden, think of making connections like an investment account. When you initially start an account, the returns that you receive as your money makes money are very small. A few cents here grows into a dollar or two there. If you were to picture this in your mind, it would look like a hockey stick. Pretty flat for a while and then BAM! **Rocket ship ROI.**

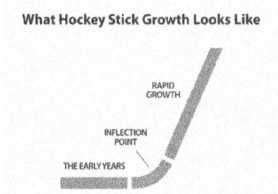

Over time, those deposits that you continue to make turn into massive returns over a long period of time and this is what I like to call "**Connection Capital.**" I have connections I've nurtured for over a decade that, once I made a "relational withdrawal" on, paid off BIG TIME (including turning into an opportunity to be hired by influencers and thought leaders Chris & Lori Harder to speak to a room full of 7 & 8 figure high-achievers, to share the stage with Dean Graziosi, who is not only a major industry giant in and of himself but he's business partners with Tony Robbins. It was an incredible opportunity – one I'm grateful to have had and I look forward to continuing to nurture those relationships for decades to come).

When you have this long term "connection capital" mindset, the way you view networking will change.

One essential aspect of this relational approach is the concept of a growth mindset—a term popularized by psychologist Carol Dweck. A growth mindset embodies the belief that abilities and intelligence can be developed over time through dedication and hard work. Networking and connecting is a learnable skill! By fostering this type of mindset in your networking efforts, you become more open to learning from others, embracing the challenges that come with learning a skill, and viewing feedback as an opportunity for improvement rather than criticism. If someone didn't resonate with your conversation at an event, it's feedback, not rejection, just like if a post you make on social media doesn't get very many "likes," it's not a rejection, it's simply feedback.

This openness not only enhances your own skills but also makes you more approachable and relatable to those around you. Every conversation and connection will provide valuable feedback as you grow.

Emotional intelligence plays a pivotal role in effective networking. It involves recognizing your own emotions as well as understanding and empathizing with the feelings of others. High emotional intelligence allows you to connect on a deeper level by being present during conversations, interpreting non-verbal cues accurately, and responding appropriately based on the emotional context of the interaction.

When I learned to take my psychology and human behavior background and pair it with connecting with someone, I learned how valuable emotional intelligence is for networking. Learning things like being a good listener, asking good questions, being present, reading people's body language and improving after each interaction can be really helpful when it comes to cultivating a great network.

Here are some tips to enhance your emotional intelligence:

1. Practice active listening: Focus fully on what others are saying without formulating responses while they speak. Be the most interested person in the room instead of the most interesting. One of my favorite phrases to use is "tell me more about that..." which invites someone to share deeper on a subject that they're passionate about. When you hold space and truly listen to someone, they will leave the conversation feeling really heard and known. And we each have a deep core need for that. When you can meet someone in a deep core need, it deepens the connection and relationship for the long term.

2. Observe body language: Pay attention to non-verbal signals that indicate how someone feels or reacts during conversations. 93% of communication is non-verbal so learning to read and understand body language is a higher level skill that will serve you as you build relationships. If you observe someone not making eye contact, that can signal that they feel more insecure or not present. If someone makes great eye contact, they tend to be more confident and engaged. If someone's arms are crossed, they may be a bit more closed off to what you're saying and if they are relaxed and open with their body language, they tend to be more open to what you're saying.

Observing body language isn't just for you to watch in others, but it's for you to observe in yourself as well. What is *your* body language portraying? Do you walk into a room confidently and taking up space, giving off an approachable yet confident presence about you or do you walk in with your head down, looking at your phone or feet with poor posture, signaling that you're less confident and less approachable?

If you're leading a community, what can you observe about yourself and others and how can you find those that may be feeling insecure and help them begin to feel more comfortable and confident within your community? Learning to read what people are saying without words is a great skill to cultivate for every area of your life.

3. Reflect on interactions: After meeting someone new or having a significant conversation, take some time to consider what went well or what could have been improved. A mentor of mine, John Maxwell, taught me about the power of reflection. You can do something but if you don't ever reflect to see what went wrong or right, there isn't any way to improve upon what happened.

Ask yourself: Was there energy and "spark" in the conversation? Did I truly listen to them? Was there no "chemistry" in a conversation and am I ok with leaving it at that? What was my body language saying? What was their body language saying? Do I view my network purely through the lens of what I can gain? Or do I appreciate how I might contribute value to those around me?

As a side not when it comes to "chemistry" with a connection, I will say that I don't base an entire relationship on chemistry. Not because it doesn't matter, but because chemistry is based on personality and personality changes. When you base a connection on chemistry, it's creating a relational-foundation on an insatiable foundation. It's like building a house on sand. Chemistry and personality will shift and change during different seasons of life (or even at different times of the month during a woman's menstrual cycle).

Some seasons may allow someone to be more outgoing and "outward facing" while other seasons they will need to be more "inward facing." I remember being in the newborn stage of having babies. It was a more "inward facing season" for me and I wasn't as social or out and about. I also didn't have as much to give during that season. If my friendships or relationships were based on my personality during that time, they would have fallen apart because I wasn't as available, I was mostly in sweat pants and figuring out what it was to be a new mom.

When it comes to the foundation of connection, instead of chemistry, I recommend building it on trust. Trust can handle the weight of changing seasons. Chemistry cannot. A relationship built on trust can have pressure put on it. Relationships built on chemistry will crumble under pressure. So network with the intent to build trust and relationship over time.

By shifting towards an emphasis on relationship-building and connection capital rather than mere transactions, you'll find that trust and stronger connections form naturally.

Consider how successful networkers tend not only to focus on their interests but also prioritize understanding others' needs and aspirations within their networks—a practice rooted firmly in empathy which cultivates trust over time.

For example, think about someone who approaches each interaction solely seeking referrals or opportunities versus another who takes genuine interest in getting acquainted with individuals beyond surface-level exchanges—perhaps asking insightful questions about their interests outside work or acknowledging shared experiences from past endeavors together (no matter how small). The latter individual is likely remembered fondly long after initial meetings because they invested time into nurturing authentic bonds. This also means being mindful of the seasons in life people are in. I remember when one of our community members was having surgery and she was going to miss our monthly event. A group of members not only helped her while she was on bed rest recovering, they brought her meals, they helped with picking her kids up from school while her husband was still at work, and we all pitched in to send her flowers. We also did a fun "*we miss you, Heather!*" group shoutout on the chapter's Instagram page and tagged her to it. This not only made a huge impact on Heather and her family, but it also allowed our members to practice what we preach within our culture.

Another part of cultivating better connections is **learning the art of asking better questions**. Did you know that most people ask the same default questions of "so, what do you do?" but over 70% of people dislike those types of questions?! I don't know about you, but I'd much rather talk about deeper topics than things like the weather. So why do we go straight to the questions that most people don't like? Because we don't have a list of better questions to ask.

If we can ask better questions, we will get better answers and create better connections. Asking better questions will not only have you create better conversations, but it will also help you stand out from other people in the room who are asking the default questions about the weather. Knowing the magic of questions, I encourage you to create a list of questions to ask. And if you're leading a community of people, teach them how to ask better questions. I do this in my community through my proprietary connection cards and teaching all of our leaders how to do this as well.

Here are some great questions to have saved in your "question bank" as you learn to **ask better questions:**

- "What initially drew you to your current profession or interest?"

- "What is life teaching you right now?"

- "What has been the biggest obstacle you've overcome, and what did you learn from it?"

- "What do you like to do in your free time?"

- "What do you think most people get wrong about you?"

- "Who is a hidden hero or role model you admire, and why?"

- "Who has had the most significant impact on your life, and how?"

If you'd like a list of **50 networking questions that create genuine connection** and keep the conversations going, visit **BusinessAndBubbly.com/questions** and download the free list.

To further support your journey toward becoming a master networker with connection capital grounded in strong relationships—and away from transactional mindsets—it's valuable here also share practical strategies aimed at enhancing these skills:

1) Mindfulness Exercises: Incorporate practices such as meditation or breathing exercises before attending events so that when entering social environments you're centered emotionally; which allows for clearer engagement. Being present is one of the greatest gifts you can give someone. I also like to say to *"leave any negativity at the door...whether or not you choose to pick them back up on your way out is up to you."*

2) Seek Feedback: Regularly ask trusted peers within your circle regarding impressions made during conversations—what felt authentic versus forced—to sharpen communication styles accordingly. Get feedback and improve along the way.

3) Set Intentions: Before going into any new social situation (whether it's virtual gatherings via online platforms or traditional meetups), identify clear intentions related specifically towards building relationships—not just initiating contact alone! Remember, it's about building relational equity and connection capital over the long term.

Ultimately mastering your approach toward effective relationship-building requires continuous reflection combined with actionable steps taken consistently across multiple interactions throughout diverse settings—from casual coffee chats all way through industry conferences!

As we continue on this journey together exploring various aspects crucial towards successful networking mastery ahead; let's keep reminding ourselves why we're here—the goal isn't simply making surface acquaintances but establishing enduring ties capable driving our careers forward collectively enriching lives along way!

Chapter Three

Understanding Your Networking Goals

In the landscape of networking, clarity of purpose is kind of like a compass for a traveler. Without it, you may wander aimlessly, collecting business cards and making small talk without any real direction or intention. This chapter is dedicated to helping you identify your personal and professional networking objectives and aligning them with your broader life purpose. By identifying clear goals, you can transform every interaction into a meaningful step toward your aspirations.

I remember when I was first starting to network, I thought it was a goal to come away from an event with the most business cards. Now, I know that's not the greatest prize. Let's dive into understanding goals and networking with intention...

To begin this journey of understanding, it's important to consider what you truly want from your networking efforts. Are you seeking new job opportunities? Looking to expand your knowledge in a specific field? Hoping to connect with mentors who can guide you along your career path? Wanting to have a specific type of referral or customer? Is there a circle of influence you want to be in? Is there an organization you want to be involved in that someone in the room is a part of?

Defining these questions will help clarify your networking goals and ensure they resonate with your larger life goals.

I remember when I wanted to connect with more leaders in my community. I got into the rooms where the leaders were meeting and then I would do what I like to call "network up." This "network up" concept means that you intentionally connect with the person in the room that intimidates you the most. This typically is one of the "bigger leaders" in the room who you may hesitate to connect with at first. This may be the event organizer, the guest speaker, or even someone who comes off very confidently. I still do this to this day because it was one of the strategies that increased my network with people of influence the quickest.

Here's what I do: I walk into a room, scan it for the people who I may feel a bit of hesitancy in approaching, I look for the event hosts and the other people who have "paid more" to be in the front row and they are the ones I go to first. Even if I feel intimidated, I take a deep breath and before my brain can talk me out of it, I approach them and begin to ask them some of the great questions I have in my "better question bank of questions." These conversations tend to turn into the best connections and conversations as well as the connections that have the largest ROI in relationships. I highly recommend doing this if you want to rapidly increase your circle of influence.

Having done this on a regular basis, what it challenged me to do was first, get out of my comfort zone on a regular basis. When we can get comfortable with being uncomfortable, little things like approaching someone no longer "feel" like a big risk. Think of it like taking your ability to get out of your comfort zone to the gym to make it stronger. Doing this "network up" not only grew my ability to take risks, it also grew my confidence.

I now have no problem walking up and connecting with anyone in any room because the "uncomfortable feeling" of taking a risk like that got smaller and smaller. It's no longer out of my comfort zone, I'm confident in speaking to anyone in any room, and I have a great network of high level leaders because of this one strategy that I've used over time. As a side benefit, this "increasing your ability to confidently take risks" also translates to other decisions you will have to make in other areas of your life. Definitely have this as one of your intentions.

Now I will say, intentions are great, but they also can be a bit "fluffy" in the way that we can "intend" to do something but not truly put it into action, so let's put this into action.

Once you've taken your intention, let's identify potential objectives. It's helpful to frame them using the SMART criteria—Specific, Measurable, Achievable, Relevant, and Time-bound. This framework serves as a great tool for goal-setting that transforms vague desires and intentions into tangible targets.

Let's break down each component of the SMART criteria:

1. Specific: Instead of stating a general goal like "I want to network more," refine it into something concrete such as "I want to connect with five professionals in digital marketing." Specificity eliminates ambiguity and focuses on precise outcomes.

2. Measurable: To track progress effectively, establish criteria that allow you to measure success. For instance, determine how many new contacts you want each month or how many industry events you'll attend over the next six months.

3. Achievable: While ambition is important, setting realistic goals is equally vital for maintaining motivation. Consider whether it's feasible given your current circumstances—time commitments or existing responsibilities—and adjust accordingly. There's a difference in being busy and being effective. Don't be busy for busy sake. This is a quick road to burnout. I've played that game and am not interested in that prize again. Be effective in your action taking, not busy.

4. Relevant: Your goals should align with both personal aspirations and professional pursuits; they need relevance in the context of where you see yourself in the future. If you're aiming for promotion within sales but are networking exclusively within creative fields, reassess those connections. If you want to network with community leaders but are in a social group for solopreneurs, you'll need to get into a different room.

5. Time-bound: Assign deadlines to create urgency around achieving these goals; without time constraints, procrastination becomes all too easy! Setting quarterly targets can encourage consistent engagement while allowing room for reflection on progress made.

As an example of applying SMART criteria effectively: if someone identifies their desire to transition into project management roles within two years but finds themselves lacking relevant connections in that field — they could set specific goals like attending one project management seminar every quarter and reaching out weekly via LinkedIn messages until they've connected with at least ten professionals working as project managers by year-end.

Reflecting on real-life cases can also shed light on successful alignment between networking strategies and career trajectories:

Consider Sarah—a marketing professional aspiring towards leadership roles who realized her network lacked individuals experienced in executive positions she wanted to reach someday; she defined her goal clearly through SMART principles by seeking mentorship from at least three senior leaders across diverse industries over six months while actively participating in two relevant conferences during this timeframe – leading not only toward invaluable insights but forming genuine relationships grounded upon learning rather than mere transactions which ultimately secured her promotion within eighteen months!

Now that we have established our approach toward setting actionable objectives let's encourage introspection regarding individual priorities:

- *What are my top three networking goals?*
- *Do these align with my long-term vision?*
- *How do I plan on measuring success?*

Take time now—write down those answers! It might seem trivial initially but articulating thoughts onto paper creates clarity previously overshadowed by uncertainty allowing greater focus when pursuing connections intentionally rather than randomly collecting contacts with no substance—a crucial distinction separating transactional interactions from relationship-building endeavors.

As we dive deeper into nurturing our newfound intentional ambitions, the next chapters will elaborate upon practical techniques—from crafting engaging first impressions through impactful pitches right down to sustaining valuable partnerships long-term!

In conclusion remember that understanding your hopes, dreams and aspirations forms a very important part when going into uncharted territories associated with cultivating connections and becoming a master networker who is building valuable connection capital.

Chapter Four

The Art of First Impressions

When you first meet someone, what do you think is the first thing that you look at? Their smiles? Eyes? Most people think that too, but in reality, we actually - in an instant - look at each other's *hands*.

Wait, what? Hands?? What do *hands* have to do with networking??

In the world of networking, first impressions serve as the critical gateway to building lasting relationships. Whether you are meeting someone for a potential collaboration, attending a conference, or simply engaging in casual conversation at a social gathering, the impact of your initial encounter can shape future interactions. This chapter emphasizes not only the importance of these early moments but also provides practical strategies to ensure that your first impression is both memorable and positive.

At the core of making an impactful first impression is effective communication. It encompasses verbal and non-verbal cues that together convey your confidence and approachability. And the first thing that we, as humans look at when someone walks into a room or walks up to us is our hands.

This goes back to "caveman days" where the hands were either signaling "friend or foe." If someone signals "friend," this comes from a palm up, or a wave where the person's palm can be seen by the other person. If someone's hands are in their pocket, crossed over their body or behind their back, our subconscious instinctually thinks *"what are they hiding?" "Do they have a weapon?" "Are they a foe?"*

If you want to make a great first impression, do a friendly wave and have both of your hands visible. This will help the other person's subconscious mind signal "friend" and not "foe."

Other things that effect a first impression is the internal confidence that you carry. Are your shoulders back or hunched over? Do you make eye contact or look down? Is your face happy and "lit up" or do you have a default "RBF" (resting bothered face). People want to connect with people who are confident in their life and business.

If you want to **grow your confidence from the inside out, take my 14-Days to Unshakable Confidence Challenge**. This online course has changed the lives of 1000+ people globally. Go to **GetUnshakableConfidence.com and use the code "fearless" for a special discount.**

Another way to make a great first impression is to come into the room or into a conversation with the mindset and energy of *"there you are!"* instead of *"here I am."* Having a *"there you are!"* mentality means that you are genuinely excited and interested to learn about someone and it sets your brain in motion to be thinking of how you can connect them with others because *"they are just the person you've been looking for!"*

Another essential tool in this arsenal of first impressions besides body language, and a *"there you are"* mindset is your elevator pitch—a succinct summary of who you are and what you do that can be delivered in about thirty seconds. Crafting an engaging elevator pitch involves identifying your unique value proposition and articulating it clearly.

Now, I know what you're thinking... "Elevator pitch? Great...I *hate* elevator pitches..."

Me too, so don't worry. I'm going to share with you one of the ways I completely changed the whole concept of the elevator pitch and made it one of the most impactful ways to share about you and your business...and trust me...you wont sound like a robot like most elevator pitches make people sound.

The elevator pitch was one of the things that repealed me from networking events. It seemed so "canned" and fake. Most people, when sharing their elevator pitch, sound like a robot and everyone listening responds with boredom. It's the typical "my name is so–and-so. My company is such-and-such and this is what I do..."

(insert *"wah-wah-wah-wah-wah-wah-wah"* sound from the Charlie Brown movie when the teacher talks).

With my background in psychology and human behavior, I knew there *had* to be a better way than the traditional elevator pitch that most networking events have. And when I found it, it changed *everything* that I do when I share during "elevator pitch time" and when I'm connecting with others. Even if I'm at another event where they do it the "normal" elevator-pitch way, I still do it "my way" because I'm not interested in being "normal." I want to make an impact and connect with people. Not blend in and be bland.

I also teach this and have my community do this within my networking events. We call it the "signature statement." It's a part of our company and community culture...Everyone *loves* it, so I know that you will too.

The concept is simple: it basically reverses *everything* that the normal elevator pitch does and it stems from how, us as humans, are *actually* wired for meaningful connection, not from the way some random sales guy thought an elevator pitch should go.

The truth is, is that *"people don't buy what you do, they buy why you do it..."* I remember hearing Simon Sinek's famous TedTalk "Start With Why" when it first came out and when he shared this quote and concept. I watched with big eyes and an open jaw when he spoke (if you haven't watched this TedTalk, stop what reading right now and watch it).

Here's the concept: Sinek's Golden Circle model consists of three concentric circles: (imagine a target sign or bullseye) - Why, How, and What. Why is in the middle circle. Then how, then what is the outside circle.

Charity Majors teaching about "Starting with Why"

Most people communicate from the outside in, starting with what they do, then how they do it, and rarely getting to why they do it. But Sinek argues that inspiring leaders and organizations do the opposite – they *start with Why*.

When applied to networking, this concept can revolutionize your elevator pitch like it has for mine and the hundreds of women who now use this within my networking company and communities.

Instead of leading with your job title or company name (the What), start with your purpose (the Why). This approach taps into the limbic brain, which is responsible for feelings like trust and loyalty. By connecting with people on this emotional level, you create a more memorable and impactful first impression.

Here's how to structure your elevator pitch using the "Start with Why" framework:

1. **Begin with your "Why"**: What's the purpose that drives you? What do you believe in? This could be a passion for solving a particular problem, a vision for change in your industry, or a deep-seated belief about how things should be done. If you start your elevator pitch with "I believe..." and fill in your "why" this is how you start with why.

2. **Follow with your "How"**: This is your unique approach or methodology. How do you bring your Why to life? How do you transform peoples lives? How do you do what you do?

3. **Conclude with your "What"**: Only after establishing your Why and How should you mention your specific role, company, or offerings.

4.

For example, instead of saying:
"*Hi, I'm Jane Smith. I'm a marketing manager at XYZ Corp. We offer digital marketing solutions for small businesses.*"
Try:
"*I believe that small businesses are the backbone of our economy and deserve the same marketing firepower as big corporations. That's why I've developed strategies to make cutting-edge digital marketing accessible and affordable for small business owners. I'm Jane Smith, and as a marketing manager at XYZ Corp, I help small businesses compete in the digital landscape.*"

This approach not only makes your pitch more engaging but also helps you connect with others who share your values and vision. It invites further conversation and creates a memorable impression that goes beyond just what you do.

Practice Exercise:

Take a moment to reflect on your own Why. Why do you do what you are doing? What drives you in your career or personal life? How can you incorporate this into a compelling elevator pitch?

Write out your Why-How-What "signature statement" and practice delivering it with authenticity and passion.

Remember, the goal of your elevator pitch isn't just to inform, but to inspire and connect.

Remember when I said that after standing up at that initial networking event and sharing my elevator pitch differently than what the event organizer taught us, but how everyone felt inspired and the energy in the room completely changed?

It's because **I started with Why.** I didn't follow the directions of the event leader...I started with why because I knew it was a better way to communicate during an elevator pitch.

By starting with Why, you're more likely to create meaningful connections that can accelerate your career and enrich your life. This "start with why" concept is what we do within my company and we are on a *mission* as an entire national team to change the way the elevator pitch is done, so if you're up for it, join with us on this quest to change the elevator pitch and **start with why!**

Now that you know the words to say as you start with why, then how, then what, remember that communication extends beyond words; body language plays an equally vital role. Your posture, eye contact, and facial expressions all contribute to how others perceive you during initial interactions. Stand tall with open shoulders—this posture conveys confidence and openness rather than defensiveness or insecurity. Maintain eye contact when speaking as well as when listening; this fosters trust and signals genuine interest.

Non-verbal cues also include gestures—using them strategically can enhance engagement during conversations. However, it's important not to overdo it; excessive gestures might distract from what you're saying rather than emphasizing key points effectively. Your nob-verbal cues and body language should support what is being said, not distract from it.

Active listening is another cornerstone skill for building rapport during initial meetings—after all, networking isn't just about showcasing yourself; it's equally about understanding others' perspectives too. When someone shares information about themselves or their work, give them undivided attention without planning what you'll say next while they're talking. This is the whole concept of **"being the most interested person in the room instead of the most interesting."**

Demonstrate active listening through paraphrasing their points back to them or asking follow-up questions that encourage deeper discussions: "*That sounds fascinating! Can you tell me more about how you approached that project?*" This practice shows engagement while allowing for richer connections between both parties involved. As you reflect back what you're hearing, understand that even if you don't get to share a lot about you or your business within the conversation, you've made a lasting impression on the person you were connecting with and that paves the way for further conversation after the initial conversation.

People will never remember what you say - they will only remember the way you made them feel. When someone feels seen, heard and known by you because you were a great listener, you asked them to expand on a topic they were sharing about and held space while sharing that you heard what they said through paraphrasing what they said, you will leave them with a lasting impression and a deep connection that will have them jumping at the chance to meet with you again.

Besides what you say and how you say it, another thing that communicates to others is the way you present yourself with what you wear.

I remember when I first started networking. I was in the fitness industry with a boutique wellness studio (remember my initial elevator pitch)?. I would pop into networking events in between client appointments but that also meant I was in my activewear and running shoes. I recognized that although my in-shape personal trailer body was great "advertising" for my services and for the gym I owned, it also didn't quite give off the energy I wanted to give off as a professional. I started bringing a change of clothes to change into before going to my networking events and would dress more professional. I began to realize that people would take me more seriously as a business owner and expert instead of the personal trainer in sweat pants.

Another concept I learned about when it comes to what you wear is called **"The Red Shoe Effect."** There was an experiment that was done with college students and their professor. One professor wore regular clothes and a regular pair of shoes and did a scripted lecture. The students were given an evaluation to answer about the professor and his material and expertise. The second set of students came into the classroom with the professor who was wearing the same set of clothes but had red shoes on instead of regular dress shoes. The professor gave the same speech and used the same material. The students were given the same evaluation but the responses from each class were very different. The students who evaluated the professor when he wore regular shoes were along the lines of not really remembering what the professor said, they had low engagement and thought his expertise and confidence was average. The students who evaluated the professor when the professor wore the red shoes - even though it was the same material - gave responses in their evaluation that signaled they remembered what the professor said, they thought he was a high level expert and really confident.

The overall lesson with this study is that if you wear something that helps you "stand out" or is different than "average" or "basic," it will actually give others a perception of you as having high confidence, that you're an expert, and they will remember what you say more!

I personally love **wearing a piece of clothing, jewelry or shoes that will help be a conversation starter.** Something that will cause someone to stop and say "OMG, I love your shoes!" (because your girl *does* love a good pair of shoes)...And with that automatic ice breaker, we can go deeper into conversation from there.

Let's recap and go over a few more quick tips for having a great first impression:

1) Dress Appropriately with a Pop: Choose attire suitable for the context in which you'll find yourself; professionalism matters in most settings but may vary depending on industry culture. And add that "pop" that will help set you apart.

2) Practice Your Pitch: Rehearse delivering your **"why-how-what" elevator pitch** until it feels natural—not overly rehearsed—to maintain authenticity. And don't be afraid to do it this way, even if the event host says differently.

3) Be Mindful Of Time: Conversations often flow more easily when there's awareness regarding appropriate timing—keeping exchanges concise shows respect toward everyone else present too!

4) Stay Calm Under Pressure: Nerves can affect performance during critical moments; consider practicing mindfulness techniques like deep breathing exercises before entering high-stakes environments.

As essential as making strong first impressions may be—their importance doesn't diminish after initial encounters are done! Continually reinforcing those positive perceptions through consistent follow-up communication solidifies connections established previously at events like industry gatherings or seminars where introductions were made earlier on.

A final aspect worth highlighting relates directly back towards evaluating your current self-presentation practices regularly over time based upon feedback you've received after various engagements—constructive criticism serves invaluable purposes here since no one becomes perfect overnight.

Mastering the art of first impressions requires intentional effort across multiple dimensions—from crafting compelling narratives around personal experiences aligning with professional aspirations right down into subtle nuances surrounding body language, clothing and choices made throughout interactions themselves.

By focusing on clear communication methods infused alongside genuine engagement strategies coupled together thoughtfully within broader contexts surrounding each encounter—you'll steadily elevate yourself into becoming someone others naturally gravitate toward wanting further relationship development opportunities along the journey!

Remember that people may not remember what you say, but they will remember the way you make them feel so be intentional with these techniques, which will help the person you're connecting with feel safe, seen, heard, and known by you.

Chapter Five

Building Your Network Strategically

Networking for the sake of networking can be fun. Especially if you're a people person. My husband, Chris, is a great connector. If you've ever taken the Gallup Strengths Finder, his top strength is called "woo," which stands for "winning others over." It literally is a strength that he has to meet a stranger and win them over into becoming a friend. He connects with everyone around him so effortlessly. He can become best friends with the teller at a bank, the bagger at the grocery store, or the lamp post on the street! He connects and networks because it's a strength of his.

Me, on the other hand, it's a skill I've had to develop. I naturally enjoy being around people, but I'm considered more of an "ambivert." It's not an introvert nor an extrovert. And just so we're clear, introvert and extrovert have nothing to do with how "outgoing" you are compared to where you get your energy from. An introvert can be a great networker as long as they've had ample time to "charge their social battery" through alone time.

As an ambivert, I can be outgoing *and* introverted. I get energy from being around certain people and other groups of people feel like they suck the life out of me and take my energy. So for me, it's not always a matter of being social compared to *who* I'm being social around. If you were to put me in a room with people talking about excel spread sheets, I would shrivel up on the inside and die (or at least that's what it would feel like). I would become so quiet, bored, and disinterested because there is nothing about excel spreadsheets that light me up on the inside. Now, if you put me in a room with big leaders talking about big ideas, plans, hopes, dreams, and goals, I will light up like the 4th of July on the inside and have so much inspirational energy to engage.

Now besides the energy of connecting, it also matters *who* you're connecting with. Chris will connect with the person bagging his groceries simply because that's a strength that he has – it comes naturally to him. I tend to have to be more intentional and strategic with who I connect with, not because I don't think the person bagging my groceries has any value to offer, but because small talk about what I'm going to cook and what my grocery list has on it drains me of my energy.

Neither way is right nor wrong. They both work great for each of us and how we are made. For me, I've had to learn how to "strategically network."

In the world of networking, the notion of chance encounters and coincidental meetings can be enticing. I've had them before where it was "just by chance" that I sat next to so-and-so on the airplane and they happened to XYZ... However, relying solely on random interactions will give mediocre results. Instead, building a network strategically is like mapping out a treasure hunt—each connection is a step closer to unlocking opportunities that can lead to career acceleration. There have been times where I've intentionally wanted to connect with a key leader or influencer in my industry and I've paid to be in their mastermind or program in order to foster that connection and the connections they have. I highly recommend doing this because these intentional investments into that connection capital also give the greatest ROI not just relationally but also related to my personal business growth.

To help you strategically develop your network no matter your personality type, we're going to explore how to assess your existing network, identify gaps, and intentionally seek out new connections that enrich your professional life.

The first step in building your network strategically is to take inventory of the connections you already have. This involves more than just listing names; it requires evaluating the strength and diversity of those relationships. Start by creating a visual representation or a mind map of your current network. Include everyone from colleagues and mentors to acquaintances and industry peers. As you compile this list, consider categorizing these individuals based on their fields, expertise, or influence in your desired area.

Once you have an overview of your existing connections, assess where there are gaps in your network. Are there industries or roles that are underrepresented? For instance, if you work in marketing but lack contacts in technology development or finance, these are areas worth exploring further. By diversifying your connections across various sectors, you not only broaden your perspective but also enhance the potential for innovative collaborations. You'd be surprised at how a concept one industry has will translate to in your own industry so fill in the industry gaps you have.

Intentionality is key when it comes to networking strategy. Rather than attending every event available or connecting with anyone who crosses your path on social media platforms like LinkedIn, focus on opportunities that align with specific goals you've set for yourself—goals we explored in Chapter 2. This requires clarity about what you want from each connection and how they fit into the larger picture of your career aspirations.

This means you can't say "yes" to every event, conference or workshop and it also may mean that you've outgrown some rooms you may currently be in. There are really great events that I would *love* to be at all the time, but when I'm focused and intentional with a goal and get honest with myself, some of those rooms aren't for me during certain seasons. Even as I write this, one of my favorite events each year is having a sale on tickets but I'm focused on different goals and connections during this season so as much FOMO (fear of missing out) as I know I will have, my goals are helping guide my decisions, not my feelings.

Another example of this that I had to learn the hard way was joining a networking group for women in business only to find out that the catch was that when you met with a member, you couldn't talk about business because they believed in creating relationships first. I agree with the relationship but it felt like a "bait and switch" because I couldn't cultivate a connection *and* talk about my business (and learn about theirs). I believe we can do both. Needless to say, I did *not* renew my membership to that particular group.

Knowing your goals, what season you're in and being intentional to fill in the gaps are helpful when it comes to strategically networking.

Here are some helpful tips when seeking new contacts within identified gaps in your network:

1. Leverage Existing Connections: One effective way to expand is by asking those already within your circle for introductions to people they know who possess skills or insights relevant to what you're seeking.

2. Attend Targeted Events: Look for industry-specific conferences or workshops where professionals gather around shared interests—the more niche the event's focus aligns with an area you're keen on exploring further.

3. Join Professional Organizations: Becoming part of associations related closely enough yet distinct from current affiliations can grant access not just through events but also through resource sharing among members.

4. Utilize Social Media Wisely: Platforms such as LinkedIn provide tools like groups and forums tailored around particular industries that allow like-minded individuals an opportunity for engagement without needing extensive prior knowledge about one another's backgrounds.

As you cultivate these new contacts while maintaining relationships with existing ones—as previously discussed—it's essential always keep an eye towards mutual benefit rather than merely transactional exchanges; reciprocity strengthens bonds over time. Connect to give *and* receive just like you must breathe in and out. It goes both ways.

Another critical aspect is understanding how different networks can complement each other effectively.

Here are helpful ways to understand:
- **Professional Networks:** These are primarily focused on career advancement—think colleagues at work or industry peers met during conferences & masterminds.

- **Social Networks:** Personal friendships often lead indirectly into professional opportunities; nurturing these ties should never be underestimated as they create bridges between different aspects of life.

- **Mentorship Networks:** Mentors offer guidance based upon their own experiences; establishing rapport here helps gain wisdom while simultaneously showcasing commitment towards growth personally/professionally through active learning efforts demonstrated during conversations/interactions together.

A key to understanding how this can work in your life is thinking about a diamond. A diamond has multiple facets that can be shown and reflected. For me, I have multiple facets to who I am as a wife, mom, CEO, former athlete, recovering plant killer, and more. I allow the facet of who I am to shine bright in specific rooms - for example: as a mom, I have an incredible network of fellow moms where we can discuss mom life, poopy diapers, some of our favorite recipes and how our kiddos are doing in school and sports. I wouldn't bring a poopy diaper conversation to a professional context unless I was intentionally trying to make someone laugh during a story. I also don't necessarily bring in depth conversation to my mom friends about social media marketing or what the latest strategy that I'm implementing within my company is, not because I'm "hiding" anything or not being authentic, I just have learned to art of knowing who I'm around and what part of the facet of who I am gets to shine.

To illustrate this concept a little further with an example, let's consider Sarah—a young graphic designer looking to land her dream job at an innovative tech startup after years spent freelancing without sufficient stability or direction professionally speaking...

Sarah begins by mapping out her current contacts—she identifies fellow designers she knows well but realizes most lack technical knowledge about coding frameworks which frequently come up when discussing potential projects within tech settings she hopes entering soon enough.

Recognizing this gap motivates Sarah into action; she attends local meetups and networking events centered around web development topics where programmers gather regularly sharing insights with each other creating supportive environments encouraging collaboration despite being in different industries. Through post-event follow up conversations she now makes with strategic connections that she knew she needed to make because of gap identification, she is able to start to nurture key connections moving forward according to her goals for her dream job.

Remember—it's not just about accumulating numbers within our lists nor chasing quantity over quality instead prioritizing depth, quality, and connection capital for the long haul. It's about finding the rooms where your "too much" is par for the course and the community that can fill in the gaps of where you feel you're "not enough." We were created for community and it takes strategic intention to build it.

Chapter Six

Leveraging Technology for Networking Success

There's nothing worse than a spam bot on social media with a canned message, so how do we leverage technology to *actually* make connections? Now, before we dive any deeper into this chapter, despite incredible options we have with technology and social media, I believe *nothing* will be able to replace heart-to-heart, belly-to-belly, business-to-business, person-to-person connection.

In today's digital age where we aren't sure if what we're seeing on Instagram is an AI robot or a real person, I believe that real in-person connections are *the* most valuable assets we can have. I also believe that the rise of AI technology and the rapid onset of digital content being available, more and more people will be awakened to how valuable human connection is so it's better to get good at it now and have the unfair advantage over others who don't know how to make and cultivate connections. Now, onto leveraging technology...

In today's fast-paced, digital world, it's no secret that the landscape of networking has transformed dramatically. What an incredible time to be alive and that we can connect with almost anyone anywhere. We aren't limited to face-to-face interactions or business cards exchanged at conferences, networking now encompasses a wide array of online tools and platforms that can significantly enhance the way we connect with others. This chapter will explore strategies for optimizing digital platforms—specifically LinkedIn—as well as effective techniques tailored to various social media audiences and approaches to virtual networking environments such as webinars and online conferences.

To begin with, **LinkedIn stands out as the premier platform for professional networking**. With over 900 million users worldwide, it offers an unparalleled opportunity to connect with industry leaders, potential mentors, and like-minded professionals. People go to platforms like Facebook and Instagram to be social and to see visual brands, but they intentionally go to LinkedIn to do business.

I'll admit, my social platform of choice is Instagram so come hang out with me there. You'll see not just things about my company but also my kids and behind the scenes of real life. Even though Instagram is *my* favorite, at the same time, I realize each platform has its own benefits and I utilize LinkedIn strategically and intentionally for industry specific connections.

People use Linkedin with the understanding that business is being done. That's not true of every other platform, despite the best efforts of every direct sales consultant trying to build a business on Facebook.

Professionals are on LinkedIn. Professionals are also on other platforms, but not specifically to do business so it's important to know where the professionals are hanging out and doing business. LinkedIn also has a higher average income over Facebook - aka if you have products and services to sell, it's likely that you will have better quality buyers who can afford your products and services that come from LinkedIn.

To leverage LinkedIn effectively, your profile must be polished and engaging. Think of your profile as your digital business card; it should reflect not just your current position but also your skills, experiences, and aspirations.

Start by ensuring that your profile photo is professional yet approachable. A smiling face helps create a sense of familiarity that encourages others to reach out. Your profile picture should show that it's you, not your cat or an artsy side-profile with your hair covering your face. It also shouldn't be a cheap selfie with bad filters. Have your profile picture be professional in nature with good lighting and only you in the image. Smartphones have nice enough camera for you to get a decent enough photo if you can't afford a professional headshot. Also know that local branding photographers tend to do what are called "headshot mini's" where they schedule a day of people to come in for 15 minutes, get a few angles of a headshot and get out. It's like a mini photoshoot that helps you get a professional headshot and a few other images without having to pay hundreds or thousands of dollars for a professional branding shoot.

I also like to leverage the LinkedIn cover photo to showcase my professional work. I suggest getting a LinkedIn layout on something like Canva, adding a few photos that "show" you doing the work you do, showcasing any press features you've had if you've had any (like a "featured in..." spot) and how you help people. If you have a lot of fancy certifications that turn into an alphabet soup of acronyms behind your name, unless your ideal audience will know what they mean, don't put them on your cover photo. Put your expertise topics and/or how you serve others and leave out the alphabet soup industry jargon. If you want to list them later in your "about" section, do that.

After having a great headshot as your profile photo and a nicely branded cover photo, next, craft a compelling headline—this is often the first thing people will see when they come across your profile. Instead of simply stating your job title, consider including keywords that highlight areas of expertise or career goals. Use ChatGPT to help you craft one if you need help or do market research and see what competitors in your industry are using as well. It's important to keep in mind that LinkedIn is also similar to a search engine so don't try and be fancy with your headline with creative names that no one else will understand. Use searchable and understandable terms that will make sense to those connecting with you and those viewing your profile.

Your summary section provides you with a unique opportunity to tell your story in a way that resonates with those who view it. Use this space not only to outline your achievements but also to express what you are passionate about in your field. This personal touch can spark interest among potential connections who share similar values or interests. I also like to add a touch of personal life and humor like me being a "recovering plant killer" and how "one of my favorite days was when my husband and children and I got to go to Africa and give 100+ pairs of shoes to underserved children in orphanages."

Don't stress about your about section. Sometimes when people are writing it, they can have an existential crisis in thinking it's permanent. It's not. You can literally add something and edit it right away. Done is better than perfect so do your best to write something professional and adjust as you learn, grow and expand along the way.

Once you have established an impressive presence on LinkedIn, it's time to start expanding your network strategically. Begin by connecting with colleagues from past jobs or internships; these individuals already have insight into your work ethic and abilities. Next, identify industry groups related to your profession where active discussions take place—joining these groups allows you access not just to information but also opens doors for meaningful conversations.

Engagement is key when building relationships online; passive profiles often go unnoticed in crowded networks. Actively participate in discussions within groups by sharing insightful articles or commenting thoughtfully on posts made by others—the goal here is visibility paired with value addition rather than self-promotion alone. Promoting your products or services isn't bad, it's only bad if it's the only thing you talk about without ever giving value and engagement. This is true for in person *and* online. Come into a room (in person and online) with a servant's heart to give, serve, offer value, and invest into your relationship bank account.

Social media extends beyond LinkedIn; platforms like X (formerly Twitter) and Instagram can play vital roles in broadening one's professional network too—but they require different approaches tailored specifically for each audience type involved.

On X and Threads (Meta's version of X)—platforms known for its brevity—engagement happens through short text posts, "threads" and replies more than lengthy discussions; knowing this, make sure to keep interactions concise but also impactful! Follow thought leaders within industries relevant both personally & professionally while interacting regularly via posts showcasing knowledge on trending topics related which could help position yourself favorably among other thought leaders over time. Personally, I enjoy using Threads, not X and tend to use Threads for quick quotes and thought leadership "nuggets of thought" vs. a lot of engagement and interaction.

Meanwhile Instagram offers visual storytelling opportunities unlike any other medium available today. Building an authentic brand becomes easier using appealing visuals alongside captions reflecting insights you may have. Like I mentioned, Instagram is my favorite platform. I think it's a great place to establish a personal brand, so if you're a rising leader, speaker or want to become a thought leader, Instagram is a great place to do that. It allows you to showcase your expertise through branded images *and* show the "personal" side of a personal brand - aka the behind the scenes of real life, which allows your audience to connect with you on a level other than a professional level. People tend to go to Instagram to see the people behind a company to see if they want to purchase something from a company. For example; if they need to go to a doctor, now a days people will go to

Instagram, not to see the company page, but to see if the doctor has an instagram account and shows up as an expert in their specialty before booking an appointment. People will buy into the vision of a leader before they buy into a product so I suggest founders, CEO's, small business owners, etc. all have an Instagram.

There are a lot of other online platforms, too many to expand on in depth in this text, but for now, you get the point. Social media is a great tool to leverage when it comes to connecting and networking. Social media isn't the only place we can connect digitally.

As a side note about social media, I want to encourage you to not rely on social media platforms for all of your communication. In the business world, social media is what we call a "rented" business asset compared to a business asset that you "own." I learned this concept the hard way when I was first starting as an entrepreneur. I spent a lot of time building a following, Facebook groups and content. Then one day, when I had tried to log in, BAM – I was BLOCKED. My account had gotten hacked. I lost access to *all* of my social media contacts, groups and ways to communicate with my customers. I eventually got it back and realized I had better start building something that I could maintain control of. This is where email lists, text lists, personal websites, blogs and podcasts come into play.

Building these other online assets are essential when building a brand, especially as you build influence and impact. We don't have time to go into building these and leveraging them in this chapter, but just know that you shouldn't rely on social media alone. Having these business assets that you own will be available no matter what the algorithm does and no matter what hot new social media platform comes out. Technology is a gift, just make sure you aren't building all of your connection capital on rented land.

With the rise of remote working arrangements comes another layer: virtual networking events such as webinars or online conferences provide excellent opportunities for connection without geographical limitations. To make the most out of these events remember two crucial elements: preparation before attending & follow-up afterward!

Preparation involves researching speakers beforehand so when questions come up during Q&A sessions, you feel informed and can engage rather than just attending as a consumer of information. Also being familiar with the type of people that will be at the virtual event helps. If you're at a virtual event for dog trainers, trying to connect with someone while talking about building furniture probably wont work.

Be engaged during the virtual event by having your camera on, being active in the chat, sending people private messages complimenting them, using reactions, and giving positive body language even on screen will help you stand out from all the other "boxes of heads" on the zoom screen. Also be sure to have a professional background behind you if you are in a professional online event and good lighting. You want to stand out to connect but in a good way.

A way to continue the conversation post event is to send personalized messages thanking speakers & fellow participants while referencing noteworthy moments that you shared during the event. This is where you take the conversation from the virtual event to either a scheduled connection call, in person coffee connect (if you're in the same town), through email or back to LinkedIn to continue the conversation. Keep in mind that online events are a "launching pad" for further connection and the ROI of relationship building is in the follow up conversations.

Remember always: technology acts merely as tools amplifying connections made organically—they should never replace genuine interactions altogether. We were created for human connection so as much as you can, leverage technology to bring connections from online to offline or at least on the phone.

Another great way to leverage online connections is by connecting in person if you travel. I have countless connections that have started online and if I travel to a city, I make sure to message them and see if we can grab coffee or meet up for dinner. It's a great way to continue to nurture your network when you finally see an online connection and get to hug them in person.

Again, nothing will replace the magic that happens when we are together in person so leverage technology as much as you can to create those genuine (and hopefully one day in person) connections.

Chapter Seven

The Power of Giving in Networking

Nothing turns people off more than the "business card speed dating" where someone comes in, shoves a business card in everyone's face and comes to simply "take" from the group. I see this with people who are just plain selfish and in it for themselves. On the other hand, I also see this with people who are new.

This is the "idea" they initially have about networking and I'm here to say it's done differently where I come from and within the community and company I've established (also why I'm writing this to hopefully shed light on how to do it the right way). I do have grace for the new people who are just learning and I hope the selfish people who come into groups to simply take and exploit them find what they're truly looking for in a different community.

As a community leader, I've set the culture of giving so that anybody who comes into our culture with a different agenda, they quickly realize they either don't fit and leave, or they adopt the culture we have set.

Networking, on the outside, can be perceived as a transactional endeavor—a series of exchanges where individuals seek to gain something for themselves. However, at the heart of effective and genuine networking lies a different principle: *the power of giving*. When we shift our focus from what we can extract from our connections to what we can offer, we create an environment conducive to building deeper, more meaningful relationships. This chapter dives into how generosity fosters stronger connections and why adopting a mindset centered around giving can lead to greater networking success.

I remember one gal who came into my networking event. She was charismatic, outgoing and promoted our group a lot on social media. She connected in the room like a champ but something in my discernment was waving an internal red-flag After a couple events, a few of my community members came up to me and asked if I was picking up on anything "off" about this individual and I shared that I had as well. My discernment had picked up and was waiting to see if she was getting involved in the community to give and to be a part or if she was trying to make as many connections that she could in order to convince our large group to vote for her during a local election. You see, she was running for a local office and kept trying to take "center stage" to talk about her platform and why everyone should vote for her.

Being the leader of the group, I had to be mindful to protect my community from being exploited and there were times when I had to kindly yet firmly step in when she was taking up space that wasn't hers to take. I was also very intentional to speak to the group at large about the culture we had as givers and not as takers. Low and behold and just as I predicted, once the election was over (which she lost), she never returned to our group.

It was evident to everyone in the community and through her actions that she was in the community to exploit it for votes and not there to give and to serve. She didn't get our votes and she didn't stick around. When there's a culture of giving, those who take will see themselves out and those a part of your culture of giving will smell a taker a mile away and not buy into their shenanigans. So be a giver when it comes to networking.

The beautiful thing about culture is that it's kind of like a thermostat. A thermostat sets the temperature of the room. If a cold wind comes in through a window, the culture will automatically adjust to go back to where its set at. Culture does the same thing for a community. When a culture is set at "giving" and creating "connection capital," when the "cold wind" of a person who is just in it for themselves comes in, our culture kicks in to set the room back to where it should be. The "cold wind" person either adapts to the temperature we have set or they realize this isn't the place for them.

If you're a community builder, I highly suggest taking this approach when creating your community culture. And if you're a networker, I recommend finding a culture that brings out the best in you!

At its core, the act of giving in networking is about creating value for others without an immediate expectation of return. Remember the whole "investing and long-term ROI" connection capital conversation earlier in the book? This concept aligns with the principle of reciprocity—when you help someone, they are likely to feel inclined to help you in return. Think about how you feel when someone goes out of their way to assist you or provides valuable information without asking for anything in return; it fosters trust and strengthens bonds.

A real life example of this is one of my dear friends, Caley. She lives out this principal in such a beautiful way that it literally turned us into some of the greatest friends. Before we knew each other, she saw a post I did on social media about a networking event I was hosting. She immediately reached out and offered her expertise as a photographer, and to take photos for our group for free. I agreed and she came. She didn't just come to take photos, she came with a heart to give and to serve. She helped with set up, tear down, content, and was one of the friendliest faces in the group, welcoming people and making them feel so loved and at home.

She came back again and did it again...and again...and again...she became known as *the* photographer to go to and she completely filled her schedule with new branding clients within a month or two. And because of her willingness to give first, it cultivated a beautiful relationship and friendship between the two of us because I *knew* she was my kind of people.

She is now one of my closest friends and it all started from her willingness to give and serve first. Be like Caley when you come into a room. Be generous. Give. Love. Serve. Be the brightest light in the room. The connection capital ROI will come back in multiple ways multiplied beyond what you may think, even beyond business. You never know the exact connection capital ROI – it could turn into tangible profit, referrals, and collaborations, but I'd have to say that deep and meaningful friendships is my favorite and most valuable ROI of all.

When I see people like this, I know *they* are my people because we share the same beliefs, which is why Caley and I are great friends and will continue to be great friends for the long term.

Know that generosity can take many forms within your network. It may involve sharing resources such as articles, books, or tools that could benefit others professionally. If you come across a webinar that aligns with a contact's interests or career goals, sending them an invitation demonstrates thoughtfulness and attentiveness toward their professional growth. I also love to do this with funny memes or little voice messages when I'm thinking of someone. I recently heard this concept called "pebbling." It comes from when penguins go out and bring back a little pebble and give it to one of their fellow penguin friends. "Pebble" your prospects and the people you are connecting with.

Another great way to give is by introducing two contacts who could benefit from each other—perhaps one seeking advice on starting a business and another with experience in entrepreneurship—can create significant value within your network. I also love introducing people who I think would get along really well because of personality, mission or even passions that I've discovered they both have.

I'm a part of a high-level networking group with other high-achievers and Brendon Burchard came in as a guest trainer for one of our events. He shared this concept, which I love how it put language into something I naturally did. He said "don't just network for you, network for your network." This means that when I'm meeting someone, I'm not just thinking about whether or not this person would be a good connection, referral or someone to do business with *for me*, I'm actually keeping in mind who else in my network this person would be a good connection for. I'm **networking for my network.**

This is a great concept to understand because as you start to connect people to people, you will become known as a connector. In my company, we love to say that "you're just one connection away" and when you can create a network where that's possible, you get *excited* to meet new people and to continue to nurture connections because you never know what that one connection could lead to!

As a community builder, I try and do this all the time. I'm constantly trying to connect people to people and one of the greatest joys as a leader is to see the connections you made begin to really flourish. I've connected people together who have gone on to be great business partners together, who have gone on to collaborate on things like podcasts, and even became best friends. To see how a connection I set up becomes the catalyst for other amazing things is so fulfilling!

In addition to tangible resources and introductions, emotional support is another powerful form of giving that often gets overlooked in professional settings. Listening actively when someone shares their challenges or celebrating their successes contributes positively to your relationship while reinforcing your role as a supportive figure within their professional journey.

When someone has something to celebrate and shares a win with you, if there's an opportunity to share it publicly, do it! For example, let's say I was connecting with Sarah at an event and she shared that she hit a huge milestone in her business. When it's my turn to share about my business or if there's time in the meeting to share about someone else, I would use that opportunity to celebrate Sarah and her accomplishment with the room. I may say something like, "before I share about my business, I want to celebrate Sarah! She hit XYZ goal so let's give her a round of applause!"

To lift someone up, recognize and celebrate them publicly is something we all need because we are *in the arena* together. The "arena" comes from a quote by Theodore Roosevelt and was made famous in our generation by Brene Brown when she wrote *"Daring Greatly"* (which is an incredible book that I highly recommend).

The quote is:

> *"It is not the critic who counts; not the man who points out how the strong man stumbles, or where the doer of deeds could have done them better. The credit belongs to the man who is actually in the arena, whose face is marred by dust and sweat and blood; who strives valiantly; who errs, who comes short again and again, because there is no effort without error and shortcoming; but who does actually strive to do the deeds; who knows great enthusiasms, the great devotions; who*

spends himself in a worthy cause; who at the best knows in the end the triumph of high achievement, and who at the worst, if he fails, at least fails while daring greatly, so that his place shall never be with those cold and timid souls who neither know victory nor defeat."

*(side note – I created a notebook with this quote on the front of it – I redid it to be the *"woman in the arena."* Grab it on Amazon if you like notebooks that inspire).

When you're *"in the arena,"* receiving recognition from a fellow person in the arena is something special. Did you know that, on average, we meet around 10,000 people in our lifetime. That's about the size of the Rome Colosseum. And I don't know about you, but I have plenty of people in the "cheap seats." In the culture we have for my community, we actually go over the concept on a regular basis and we emphasize that we are each other's biggest fans, not the ones in the cheap seats so we celebrate and encourage each other.

Whether you're a community builder or a connector, I highly suggest adopting this principal. People will notice and this will help continue to change the culture of networking for the better.

By embracing this spirit of encouragement, celebrating others and generosity, you'll not only enhance their personal brand but also cultivate an ecosystem where everyone feels empowered and valued. When people perceive you as someone who genuinely cares about advancing others' interests—not just your own—they are more likely to engage with you authentically and reciprocate whenever possible. You *will* reap what you sow.

To harness the full potential of giving within your network, consider these practical strategies:

1. Identify Opportunities for Contribution: Regularly assess how you might help those within your network by keeping track of ongoing projects or developments they share on social media platforms like LinkedIn or during casual conversations at events.

2. Create Value-Driven Content: Share insights through blog posts or social media updates that address common pain points within your industry; this not only positions you as an authority but also provides helpful information others can leverage.

3. Offer Your Expertise: Volunteer time for mentorship opportunities either formally through structured programs or informally by inviting less experienced professionals out for coffee chats where knowledge exchange occurs naturally.

4. Follow Up Thoughtfully: After meeting someone new at an event or conference—and especially if you've committed any form of assistance during that encounter—make sure that your follow-ups express genuine interest while reminding them you're available if they need further support down the line.

5. Lift others Up - When given the opportunity, celebrate those around you and lift them up. The rising tide lifts all ships so don't just be a ship waiting for the tide to rise. Be the tide. Encourage them.

Celebrate their wins. Be their biggest fans because you are all in the arena together.

As we adopt these practices grounded in generosity into our networking approach, it's essential also not just focus solely on individual relationships but recognize collective gains achieved through collaboration across networks too! Some of the greatest connections come from intentional collaboration.

In the television industry, they call this "cross-pollination." For example: if you've ever seen one of the detective shows that has one of the characters from the firefighter show that also makes an appearance in the police show, this is what cross pollination is. As you watch the show, you get hooked on one of the characters and before you know it, you're not only watching the detective show but you're also watching the firefighter show.

The television show producers understand that you, as the viewer of the detective show, you're an "ideal viewer" for the police and firefighter shows. *You* may not know it yet because you're so loyal to your detective show, but once you watch that firefighter character on the detective show, you realize "hey, I want to know what's happening with that story line of the firefighter" so you start to watch the firefighter show.

Youtubers are also really great at this. Having kids myself, I see this with toddler shows on a regular basis. Ms. Rachel will bring on The Wiggles and Blippi and after seeing that one episode of Ms. Rachel, she now wants to also watch The Wiggles *and* Blippi because she loved them on the Ms. Rachel show.

You can also do this not just with people but with products. For example: Baby Einstein (yes, we're sticking with the toddler theme), does this in the way that they show kids playing with toys. Guess what they have on their website? The toys from the show that you can purchase.

If you can take this same "cross-pollination" concept into the business world and make key collaborations, you'll achieve some really great momentum as you "scoop up" a whole new audience or make extra income by becoming an affiliate from someone else's product or service?

Here are some ideas for collaboration with your network:

- Hosting joint events that cultivate collaboration among different industries. This strengthens cross-pollination while increasing visibility and benefiting all participants involved.

- Promoting a product or service that compliments your business. This helps support those who know, like and trust you with their pain points while also creating deep bonds of support with the other business or person that you're promoting.

- Engaging actively within community organizations. Show up to someone's business ribbon cutting ceremony. Volunteer at a non-profit organization. Host an event at a small business' space and bring new customers and awareness to their business. Things like this create the cross-pollination effect where everyone wins.

This doesn't mean that you do everything for everyone... it means that as you give and collaborate, notice who also gives and collaborates in return. This doesn't mean that you do something *expecting* to get something in return. It means that you're aware of who else has the heart to serve and collaborate vs. those who are just there to take and never give back.

In situations where I've given and collaborated and it wasn't reciprocated, I tend to not nurture and foster those relationships as much not because I don't find the person valuable, but because their actions show me that they aren't in a place to cultivate a mutually-beneficial connection.

Nurturing relationships built upon reciprocity leads us towards fulfilling long-term partnerships rather than superficial connections formed purely based on convenience alone—which rarely contribute significantly toward career acceleration or win-win situations.

Ultimately, when you lead with a heart to give and serve throughout professional interactions, you will cultivate trust and a great reputation within your network. By prioritizing value addition over transactional exchanges and creating win-win collaborations, you will become known within your network and create not just great professional connections but personal friendships as well.

Chapter Eight

Maintaining and Nurturing Relationships

Have you ever met someone and had a great connection, only to never hear from them again? Have you ever met someone and had a great connection and you followed up with each other and continued to foster the connection and it was great?

How did you feel during the different interactions? I bet that if you saw the "never heard from again" person out and about, you would feel awkward and so would they, compared to the person who you followed up with.

The truth is, connections need nurturing. The other truth is that most people are waiting for someone else to go first with the follow up. So *you* go first.

In the intricate dance of networking, establishing connections is only the first step. It is the nurturing and maintenance of these relationships that transforms surface encounters into lasting connections. This chapter emphasizes why ongoing relationship management is crucial for success in both personal and professional realms.

The importance of follow-ups, thoughtful communication, and consistent engagement cannot be overstated; they are the lifeblood of a thriving network. This is where you start to add deposits to the connection capital.

To begin with, let's revisit the idea that networking should be viewed as relationship-building rather than a transactional process. When we meet someone new at an event or reach out via social media, our initial interaction might spark a connection. However, without deliberate effort to nurture this bond, it risks fading into obscurity among countless other contacts we accumulate over time.

Just like the garden analogy, if you never water your plants, they will shrivel up and die. As a recovering plant killer, I know this all too well!

The key to maintaining relationships lies in understanding that *each* connection has its own unique value proposition—each person you meet can potentially offer insights, opportunities, or support throughout your career journey. And yes, when I say "each connection," I mean it. Don't discount anyone and don't judge a book by its cover. Each person has value and you never know their story, who they are connected to, and how mutually beneficial a connection can be. I've found that sometimes the people "hiding in the corner" of a networking event have the most value to add. Not to discount the ones in the room that "stand out," but to also elevate the quieter ones or the ones that don't stand out in the crowd as much.

To cultivate these connections effectively, you must be intentional in your approach. Just like watering your garden takes intention, so does cultivating and nurturing connections.

One useful framework for relationship maintenance is learning **the CONNECT acronym:**

Connect-Offer-Nurture-Notify-Engage-Communicate-Team.

- **Connect:** Establishing contact after meeting someone should be prompt *and* genuine. Within 24 to 48 hours after your first encounter—a conference chat or coffee meeting—send a personalized message expressing gratitude for their time and referencing specific elements from your conversation that resonated with you. This not only reinforces their significance but also sets the stage for future interactions. I like to use voice messages for this since it's a better form of communication over just text on a screen.

- **Offer:** Consider how you can provide value to your network members regularly. This could involve sharing relevant articles tailored to their interests or inviting them to events that align with their professional pursuits. By being proactive about offering assistance or resources without expecting immediate returns, you cultivate that relationship capital within your network.

- **Nurture:** Over time, make it a habit to check in on individuals at intervals appropriate for each relationship's context—this could range from monthly messages for close ties to quarterly emails for more distant acquaintances. Inquire about updates in their lives or careers and share some of yours as well; this back-and-forth fosters deeper connections while keeping everyone informed about one another's journeys.

- **Notify:** Keeping your contacts updated on significant developments in your professional life helps maintain relevance within those relationships. Whether it's landing a new job, achieving a milestone project completion, hitting a goal or speaking at an industry conference—these moments are worthy notifications! They serve as touch points sparking further conversations while reinforcing mutual interest.

- **Engage:** Interaction should never feel one-sided; encourage dialogue by asking open-ended questions during conversations that invite others' input on various topics related both personally and professionally. Demonstrating genuine curiosity fosters trustworthiness—the foundation upon which strong networks thrive! Ending your side of the conversation with a question is a valuable skill to implement, wouldn't you agree? (see what I did there)?

- **Communicate:** Adaptability is vital when communicating across different platforms—whether through email newsletters designed specifically for sharing insights among colleagues or casual messages exchanged via social media channels like Instagram or LinkedIn where brevity matters most. Tailor each communication method appropriately so recipients feel valued rather than overwhelmed by excessive information.

- **Team:** Collaborative and "cross-pollination" efforts often produce fruitful results—and they aren't limited solely within formal work environments. Consider teaming up with selected individuals from your network on projects aligning around mutual goals; whether leading workshops together helping others build skills relevant today's market demands OR launching community initiatives focused towards causes close to both of your hearts will create stronger bonds while also amplifying impact.

While following this "CONNECT" model enhances relational dynamics throughout networks cultivated over time—the art of connection lies within the understanding of emotional intelligence (EI). Emotional intelligence reflects our ability to accurately discern emotions within our own personal world as well as discerning where someone else may be. The emotional *"intelligence"* part goes into not just the proper interpretation of those but also making sure our responses from the point of interpretation is positive and favorable.

Someone with high emotional intelligence and a strong "internal world" can take any bad situation, interpret it in a positive way and make it better. Is life happening *to* you or *for* you? Do you see challenges in front of you and become a victim of the circumstance or do you see the challenge as a way to grow? Strong emotional intelligence will help you with this.

To enhance emotional intelligence consider practicing active listening techniques during conversations—pay attention not just verbal cues but non-verbal signals too like body language tone, and voice inflection. Reflecting back what you've heard ensures clarity comprehension allows parties involved feel heard validated and fosters deeper connections.

Another form of emotional intelligence means that you are also responsible for the energy that *you* bring to the conversation. If you've had a hard morning, do you complain or verbal vomit negativity all over the person you're connecting with or do you turn that hard morning around, find the lessons you are learning and share from a place of overcoming a challenge?

Being responsible for the energy you bring into a room or conversation means you don't let negative experiences "bleed out" over those around you. It means you don't let a negative experience change your attitude into a negative attitude and then you bring your negative attitude into the conversation with others.

High emotional intelligence doesn't mean you ignore your feelings, it means that you don't let them drive you. Emotions is the language of the heart but they are meant to be passengers, not drivers. Your values and goals should drive you, not emotions. You may *feel* frustrated, but holding a higher value of being kind to someone means that you deal with your frustration on an internal level or with specific people that know they are helping you process frustration so that doesn't "come out" on someone else.

Some people don't understand this concept, especially in a world that has a lot of emphasis on *how we feel*. The truth is, feelings can be fickle and they are fleeting. Our feelings are valid *and* what matters more than our feelings is what we do with them and how we respond.

So be responsible for the energy that you bring into a conversation or into an event. If you want a deeper understanding on this, I go further into detail in my other book, "Meant For More; Igniting Your Purpose in a World that Tries to Dim Your Light." I highly suggest reading it.

As we conclude this exploration into maintaining relationships, remember successful networking isn't merely about accumulating names or followers on social media, but creating bridges that are built on authenticity, generosity, shared experiences and cultivating growth together. Embrace every opportunity to connect and nurture those connections.

It will be one of the things that heals lonely hearts AND propels you into your future. I believe that as our world rockets into a digital and AI age, more and more people will be awakened to the value of human connections, networking and cultivating community. And not just "networking how its always been done," but networking for genuine connection.

The last thing I'll close with is that networking deals with people. People are beautiful and messy at the same time and when you can come to the table with a heart to serve, love and give, whatever your journey is with networking, remember this beautiful quote from Mother Theresa:

We were never meant to do business or life alone and we were created for community.

And always remember, *you're just one connection away...*

Chapter Nine

Shift the Networking Culture with Us!

If you're here at the end, congratulations! I hope this book gave you a deeper understanding as well as practical strategies that will help you become a master connector and networker that cultivates a thriving community.

My hope is that whether you're a connector or community builder, you use these insights to shift the culture of networking for the better.

If you want to get involved in one of our networking events and connected with an incredible community, head over to **BusinessAndBubbly.com** to find a chapter near you.

If you don't have one near you or maybe you're interested in not just *being in the room* but **leading the room,** being a Chapter Director could be for you!

You will learn how to speak, facilitate, lead and build other women up while implementing our "Profitable Community Blueprint" as you nurture a healthy culture of connection and community in your local area. We have an incredible community of directors who are all on this mission together. We are a part of something bigger than what we could ever do by ourselves so if this is you, we'd love to chat!

Go to BusinessAndBubbly.com and click the "apply to be a chapter director" button to learn more.

We are on a mission to cultivate genuine connection on a global scale and we know that we can't do it alone. We believe that we have a piece of this grander puzzle so come be a part of something that's bigger than what you could ever do on your own and let's be a part of the solution the world is waiting for – together.

Cheers to your success!

PS – come connect with me on Instagram or LinkedIn...but really...I'd love to connect with you! I'd love to hear what your favorite takeaways are and how you're cultivating connection and community around you, and if there's anything I can do for you or anyone I can connect you with. I can be found at @CharityMajors on all platforms or on my website CharityMajors.com

Chapter Ten

About Charity Majors

As a seasoned leadership and team-building expert, Charity Majors helps organizations unlock the power of their people through customized training programs and executive coaching.

With a corporate and collegiate background in creating corporate programs, hiring, team building, and company culture, Charity brings a deep expertise in human behavior, communication, and leadership.

Charity's proprietary frameworks, including the Major Impact MESSENGER, The A.C.E. Connection Effect, the Major Impact

LEADERSHIP Accelerator, The CONNECT Effect and The Profitable C.O.M.M.U.N.I.T.Y. Blueprint, combine proven methodologies with cutting-edge insights from human behavior and communication.

These frameworks have helped numerous people and organizations improve employee engagement, boost productivity, teamwork, communication and cultivate a culture of high performance.

As an award-winning entrepreneur, speaker, and author, founder/CEO, Charity Majors has spoken on international stages to thousands of people and has impacted lives globally for over a decade.

With multiple degrees and a robust background in leadership development, Charity is well-equipped to tailor offerings to each organization's unique needs.

Charity's approach focuses on building meaningful connections, fostering healthy communication, promoting commitment, ensuring growth and development, and creating a positive and supportive culture.

By emphasizing care, connection, communication, commitment, valuable content, growth pathways, conflict resolution, emotional intelligence and a culture of trust and honor, Charity helps leaders and teams navigate complex challenges and thrive in today's fast-paced business landscape.

With a commitment to developing leaders rather than followers, Charity empowers organizations to create environments where people can grow, contribute, and achieve their full potential.

Whether you are a Fortune 500 company or a growing collegiate community, Charity Majors is the trusted partner you need to drive measurable results and build a thriving culture.

Learn more at CharityMajors.com

Chapter Eleven

Acknowledgements

It's only fitting to close this book with gratitude for my people...

First and foremost, **thank you Jesus** for being the ultimate connector and creating us for community. What an honor it is to carry this message to the ends of the earth and to follow your example. May you receive your full reward through me as we shift culture and live out the kingdom mission of *"in community as it in in Heaven..."*

To my husband: thank you for being not only one of my greatest teachers in learning healthy connection but also one of my biggest fans. As we've grown together in the ways we connect and communicate, I've been able to translate that into cultivating healthy community. They say "iron sharpens iron" and I'm glad we've had sparks fly that sharpen each other. Thank you for believing in me, encouraging me, sharpening me and always pointing me to Jesus. I am so grateful for you and our love.

To my babies: Judah and Eden, you are my heart walking on the outside of me. You teach me more than you know and I am forever honored to have been chosen as your mommy. Thank you for the opportunity to unconditionally love and to have a connection that goes beyond eternity and life itself. I love you 9498249957299275892847568290284757893029272666587599 0infinity98274859973626927759497228945788275789928757939 02758infinity208575789903927277595098947728 9infinity0927475894927785949 7foreverandeverinfinity.

To my best friends, Lyndsie, Caley, Viorica and Aimie: thank you for being you and loving me. Your friendships mean more than words could ever express. The way we've traveled through different seasons together, grown, had disagreements, laughed until our bellies hurt and cried until we had no more tears, I am eternally grateful. Thank you for being my people through thick and thin and being in it for a lifetime of friendship.

To my Business & Bubbly Chapter Directors: thank you for your "yes" to join me on this journey of cultivating incredible communities all around the world! You carry such a special piece of this larger puzzle and none of us would be making the collective impact we are making if we weren't building this thing together. Your heart for community is what helps me keep going even when it gets hard and I am continuously inspired by each of you!

To our Business & Bubbly community: YOU are the real MVP's! Thank you for being a part of this grand mission and for being a special piece to each local chapter. YOU are a big part of what makes this whole thing so special...we truly *are* better together, now let's go change the world!

www.ingramcontent.com/pod-product-compliance
Lightning Source LLC
Chambersburg PA
CBHW070550030426
42337CB00016B/2428